Dr. Gwen's A to Z Self-Care Guide To New Beginnings

Gwendolyn A. Martin, Ed.D., LPC

Also by Dr. Gwen

FREE YOUR MIND

(Journal)

IMPORTANT NOTE TO READERS: This book has been written and published for informational and educational purposes only. It contains advice related to self-care and should be used as a supplemental resource. This book is not intended to diagnose or treat any medical condition and is not a substitute for seeking the advice of a physician or another trained health professional. Do not stop, start, or change any prescription medication, medical treatment, or program without consulting your doctor. Any use of information in this book is made on the reader's sound judgment and is the reader's sole responsibility.

All Rights Reserved

No part of this book may be reproduced or used in any form or manner without prior written permission of the copyright owner, except for the use of quotations in a book review.

Copyright © 2023 by Gwendolyn A. Martin

ISBN-13: 978-1-7364413-8-1

Dedication

This book is dedicated to ALL who aspire to RISE, REFLECT, and REFORM, thereby living more purposefully and productively.

My Message

New beginnings can be challenging, heartbreaking, and a huge blow to your ego depending on the circumstances surrounding your need for a fresh start. Sometimes starting over can be by choice, and other times the choice is made for you. Either way, you have some control over how you proceed. New beginnings often require you to humble yourself and take a step back to regroup. It doesn't matter if it is starting a new relationship, career, life after divorce, getting clean, or being freed from incarceration; I suggest focusing on the things you can control, like your mindset, attitude, and energy.

Starting over isn't always about failure or loss. It's more about realizing that you are worthy and deserve better, even if you are not fully aware of what better entails. Think about starting over as a fresh start by learning from the past and using the knowledge and experience you've gained over the years to catapult you into the life you dream of, desire, and deserve. A new beginning is going to take a lot of strength, courage, patience, and commitment. Get ready because it is not going to be easy. Nothing worth having ever is. Just ask any successful person how many times they failed before they finally got it right. However, the freedom and sense of accomplishment a new beginning can bring are worth the struggle. Yes, the struggle is real!

Introduction

I am delighted to share Dr. Gwen's A to Z Self-Care Guide to New Beginnings. I know that hitting that reset button and starting over from square one is scary. Just the thought of having to encounter some of the same obstacles you successfully navigated in the past is sickening. **However, don't beat yourself up, and don't view starting over as punishment. You've punished yourself enough. Everyone else has too. Instead, view your new beginning as a way to improve your quality of life and start living more purposefully and productively.** After all, you've done it before and can do it again. This time you will be armed with more knowledge, skills, and strategies to help you sustain and achieve desired results.

Dr. Gwen's A to Z Guide to New Beginnings is designed to help you get unstuck and take those initial first steps to a new, improved, better YOU. I plan to help you use what you know best: YOU! We are all on a journey to finding the best version of ourselves. You are not alone. Self-care is a great place to start improving your overall mental health and well-being. This guide contains some powerful, effective, practical self-care tips and solutions that can easily be incorporated into your existing daily routine. Self-care is about regularly engaging in deliberate activities and practices to reduce stress, control emotions, improve communication, decrease verbal and physical aggression, and respond better to difficult situations. Self-care will help you engage in more activities that make you feel happy, connected, and supported. As a result, you will boost your physical, mental, and emotional health. Focus on making small improvements daily. Each change you make moves you closer to living your best life. Dr. Gwen's Self-Care Tips, included throughout the book, will guide you in shifting your mindset and perspective. **Remember, you are in charge of your life, and YOU determine how your story ends. So, let's make it a happy ending.**

Contents

2 Future-Self Love Letter

9 A – D

25 E – H

38 I – L

55 M – P

69 Q – S

79 T – W

96 X – Z

106 Afterwards

113 Self-Care Pledge

115 Self-Care Check-Up

118 Acknowledgements

119 Book Review

SELF

Change your mindset and attitude.

Ask for help when needed.

Rest, release, recharge, renew.

Eat healthy and exercise regularly.

Future Self Love Letter

Today is a new beginning. Together we are going to make sure that you **RISE, REFLECT, and REFORM** as you uncover and reveal the new and improved YOU! As you embark on this self-care journey, the first thing we are going to do is take some time to assess where you are at this moment and where you would like to be (your dream come true) by writing a Future-Self Love Letter to yourself. Because you are motivated, inspired, and committed to self-improvement, several pages are dedicated solely to this purpose. **YOU ARE WORTHY** and deserve to be healthy and happy in every aspect of your life.

While writing this Future-Self Love Letter, take time to pause, reflect, express gratitude, show appreciation for who you are, and set future goals (big and small) that will bring you closer to realizing your dream life. This letter will give your life purpose, develop a clear vision of what you want to achieve, and help you create an action plan.

Writing a Future-Self Love Letter is empowering. It will improve your mood, reduce stress and anxiety, provide accountability, and increase your likelihood of success. As you begin writing, take a moment to reflect on why you decided NOW is the time to make changes in your life. Be open, transparent, and nonjudgmental of your feelings, ideas, hopes, and dreams as they surface. Get it all out — release and let go! After completing this guide, as you continue your journey, look back and reflect on the progression...challenges, and triumphs.

Here are a few writing prompts to get you started:

- Dear future self...

- In five years...

- My new beginning starts today by...

Don't be a prisoner
of your past mistakes.
Use them as
growth opportunities.

A

Ask for help,

not because

you are weak,

but because

you want to remain

STRONG.

~ Les Brown

A – Ask for Help

Do you have a hard time asking for help, even when you desperately need it? I see it all the time in my career as a teacher and counselor. Children and adults often need help but don't ask for it. Sometimes, even when support is offered, they won't accept it. At the end of the day, a lot of time is unnecessarily wasted, and they struggle needlessly.

Some people are reluctant to ask for help because of their pride, ego, thoughts about letting others down, fear of being judged, wanting to do it themselves, or just not wanting to draw attention to themselves. When did asking for help become a sign of weakness? Let that misconception go. Others fear rejection, tend to underestimate peoples' willingness to provide assistance or support and overestimate how inconvenienced people would feel when asked for help, according to a Stanford University team study in Psychological Science.

If I'm being honest, I've had my own struggles with asking for help. There are times when I'm reluctant and feel uncomfortable asking for help. I have a strong independent GIRL POWER personality. Since I was a little girl, it's been a source of pride to do things independently. I can be a bit of a control freak at times. I find comfort in knowing that I don't have to depend on others to succeed. Sometimes it feels easier to shoulder the burden by myself. I'm in complete control. As I've gotten older and wiser, I realize that there are people out there who have traveled the roads I'm traveling and can help me navigate obstacles and prevent me from wasting time even if I can get the job done single-handed. I understand that help is only a text, an e-mail, a phone call, or a visit away. There are people out there who want to help you, who will help you, all you have to do is say the word – HELP! Ask for help whenever you feel stress or strain about anything in your life – your home, your work, your family, your relationship, your health, your finances, etc. Sometimes a small problem can become a much bigger problem when we try too hard and too long to work things out on our own. Let others help you cope successfully with the circumstances of your life. Have the courage to begin again.

Dr. Gwen's Self-Care Tip:

Here are some things to keep in mind when asking for help:

1. It's best to ask for help in person or call the person if possible. Text and e-mails are often misconstrued, and it's easier for people to say no when they don't understand what you need.

2. Be direct and specific about what you need.

3. Communicate what you have done to try to solve the problem yourself. People are more apt to help you if they know you are trying to help yourself.

4. Understand that most people enjoy helping others and want you to succeed.

Make a list of people you can ask for help and call on for support.

Family:

Friends:

Colleagues:

Spiritual Leaders:

Mentors:

Coaches:

Community Leaders:

Counselors:

Educators (Current or Past Teachers and Administrators):

B

Take a deep breath,

pick yourself up,

dust yourself off,

and start all over again.

~ Frank Sinatra

B – Box Breathing

Breathing exercises are a great way to lower blood pressure, regulate our emotions, and relax after a stressful day. Breathing exercises can be practiced routinely every day, or you can do them when your feelings are heightened.

Here is one of my favorite breathing exercises.

Box Breathing

Box breathing, also known as square breathing, is a type of rhythmic deep breathing technique that can reduce stress, calm your body, and relax your mind. To practice box breathing:

1. Inhale slowly through your nose for a count of four. Let the peace in your breath flow to your mind, body, and soul.
2. Hold your breath for a count of four.
3. Exhale slowly through your mouth for a count of four. Release all thoughts that cause stress, tension, and anxiety in your body.
4. Pause for a count of four.
5. Repeat steps 1-4 three to five times or until you start calming down.

One of the great things about box breathing is that it can be practiced anywhere, anytime – sitting in a chair, lying in bed, watching tv, in crowded places, or even while bathing. So, whenever you need to re-center yourself, concentrate, or find yourself in a stressful situation, box breathing is a simple, effective calm-down strategy.

Give Box Breathing a try!

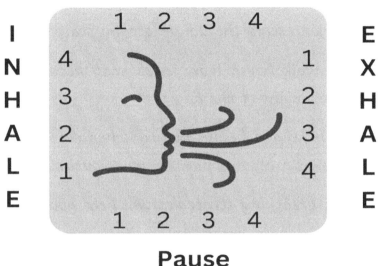

Dr. Gwen's Self-Care Tip:

Make it a daily practice to stop several times throughout the day and JUST BREATHE!

Start first thing in the morning during your daily affirmations. As the saying goes, you can kill two birds with one stone. Continue to take deep breaths during lunch to give your brain a break and again at night before bed to help you relax and prepare your body for sleep.

Creatively find ways to consistently incorporate deep breathing into your daily schedule. Here are a few additional suggestions:

1. Place a post-it note on your bathroom mirror as a reminder to start the day with a few deep breaths while in the shower or getting dressed for work.
2. Take a few moments to do some deep breathing when you first arrive at work to start the day in a calm state.
3. The drive or walk home from work may be an optimal time to release all the weight of the day.

In the beginning, it might be helpful to schedule reminders on your phone until it becomes a regular part of your routine.

Practicing effective breathing strategies will help you reduce stress and maintain calm. Use deep breathing to free yourself from thought patterns that make you feel vulnerable and weak.

Try these FREE apps for additional breathing exercises:

Calm

Headspace

MyLife

iBreathe

BREATHE

It's only a bad

Moment,

Hour,

Day,

In time.

It's not a bad life.

YOUR BOUNCE-BACK GAME IS STRONG!

C

A bad attitude
is like a flat tire,
you won't get anywhere
unless you change it.

~ Unknown

C – Commit to Change

Change is a daily, weekly, monthly, and yearly process. Change can gradually improve old habits, overcome challenges, and slowly manifest your hopes and dreams. A positive mindset and attitude are what separates the best from the rest. On the other hand, a bad attitude can be your downfall. As the old folks would often say, **don't block your blessings**. A bad attitude can also block you from receiving love and light in your life. It does not matter how much time you have wasted, do not blame others or your circumstances. Start taking responsibility for your actions and poor decision-making. You can always start over, make a change, and do better. You deserve a life of happiness and positivity.

Your commitment to change should be based on your perceived benefits and values. Only YOU can change your life for the better. For example, you are the only person who can change your thoughts, habits, make amends, communicate your needs, etc. Consider the person who just got diagnosed with a life-threatening illness, got fired from their job, got served divorce papers, or was sentenced to a five-year prison sentence. In each case, the person is faced with a new beginning that requires them to decide how to live their life moving forward.

Once you commit (dedicate yourself to something or someone), there will be people, places, and things you will need to leave in the past. Don't continue to carry the extra weight of toxic people, denial, regret, guilt, sadness, and fear. Instead, acknowledge and make peace with the past. You can't change it, but you don't have to let it hold you back either. However, you can forgive yourself and others and start transforming into the person you want to become in the future. Over time, your past will fade and truly become a thing of the past, a testimony.

Dr. Gwen's Self-Care Tip:

Here are three steps that can help you when making a commitment to change.

1. **Be Specific** – Clearly identify the change to be made.

2. **Consequences** –Think about the positive and negative consequences of the commitment to change that you have made. For example, what kind of support will you need, who will provide the support, etc.?

3. **Benefits** – Remind yourself daily of the positive impact the changes you are making will have on your life, personally and professionally.

It doesn't matter

how much time

you've wasted,

there's always time

to make a change

and strive for more.

D

Sometimes you need to
distance yourself
to see things
more clearly.

D – Distance

Sometimes it is necessary to distance yourself or, in other words, wash your hands or disassociate from people, places, or things, as mentioned before, that does not align with the new and improved YOU. **For example, if there's physical or verbal abuse, if the relationship is causing you undue stress and anxiety, or if you've noticed a change in your mood when around a particular person due to attitude, disrespect, lying, or putdowns. These are just some of the reasons why it may be time to consider detaching yourself physically and emotionally from those people and relationships.** Don't let someone drain you or, as I like to say, suck the life right out of you and wreak havoc on your physical, emotional, and mental health. You have the power and the right to protect your peace.

Dr. Gwen's Self-Care Tip:

Inner peace and unlimited opportunities await you when you distance yourself from negativity, drama, and joy jackers.

Make a list of the people, places, and things you need to distance yourself from and stop giving energy to as you transition into the person you are destined to become. Make a note of why you need to distance yourself as a reminder to make yourself a priority.

PEOPLE	WHY?
PLACES	WHY?
THINGS	WHY?

E

Exercise not only changes your body. It changes your mind, your attitude, your mood.

E – Exercise/Physical Movement

Exercise is a healthy way to use your body to express what is going on inside of you and to reduce anxiety and stress. Studies have shown that exercise has many positive benefits on our physical and mental health. Physically, exercise helps you lose weight, increases muscle, and improves your sex life. Mentally, exercise reduces symptoms of depression, boosts self-esteem, increases creativity, etc. According to the American Heart Association, at least 150 minutes (2.5 hours) of heart-pumping physical activity per week can help you think, feel, and sleep better and perform daily tasks more efficiently. Additional benefits can be gained from being active for at least 300 minutes (5 hours) per week. However, increasing the amount and intensity gradually over time is recommended. Don't worry; your physical activity does not have to be running a marathon; it can be something such as leisurely walking, a light jog, strength training, or flexibility training. Health professionals recommend exercising four to five days a week.

Dr. Gwen's Self-Care Tip:

Here are some exercises you can start incorporating into your daily self-care routine.

What kind of exercise do you enjoy the most? Why?

What kind of exercise do you like the least? Why?

Cardio Training	Strength Training	Flexibility Training
Walking	Push-ups	Yoga
Running	Pull-ups	Pilates
Basketball	Squats	Tai Chi
Tennis	Lunges	Resistance Bands
Soccer	Bench Press	Stretching
Cycling	Weight Machines	
Hiking	Barbells	
Dancing	Burpees	

F

Success is not final.

Failure is not fatal.

It is the **COURAGE** to continue that counts.

~ Winston Churchill

F – Failure Is an Opportunity for Improvement.

Is the fear of failure keeping you from progressing? Are you afraid to take risks and step outside your comfort zone? Fear of failure will keep you unhappy in your current life struggle. Don't view failure as a measure of our worth, a sign of weakness, or an indication that you are not capable of making your wildest dreams come true. Get back up, dust yourself off, and try again. Let's start viewing failure as a new beginning and a chance to start over and do things better. Successful people view failure as learning and growth opportunities. They are transparent and open to sharing that they got it wrong many times before finally getting it right. Successful people share how they capitalized on their failures, used them as growth opportunities, and did not give up when encountering roadblocks and setbacks. Don't let failure stop you from accomplishing your dreams.

Dr. Gwen's Self-Care Tip:

Michael Jordan is just one example of someone who set high expectations for themselves and persevered. He is undoubtedly one of the greatest basketball players of all time. Here is what he said about succeeding. *"I've missed more than 9000 shots in my career. I've lost almost 300 games. 26 times, I've been trusted to take the game-winning shot and missed. I've failed over and over and over again in my life. And that is why I succeed."*

Questions to consider after a failure:

1. **Are my expectations/goals realistic?**
   I know you have heard the saying you must crawl before you walk. You can't start out running. In other words, sometimes, we set our initial goals too high and don't give ourselves the time or grace we need to succeed. Cut yourself some slack. Break your goals down into smaller, more achievable pieces.

2. **What can I do differently?**
   Take time to reflect on what went well and what was an epic failure. View outcomes as minor setbacks. Think about what you can do differently the next time around. Knowledge is power. Small tweaks and changes can make a world of difference.

3. **Do I have a growth mindset?**
   Are your vibes positive, or is negative self-talk keeping you grounded in fear and doubt? Monitor your thought life. For example, please don't say things like I can't do this... I'm not good enough or smart enough...I suck! Instead, tell yourself that you are getting a little better each day. Remember, failure is an opportunity for improvement.

4. **Who can help?**
   Have you asked for help, or better yet, have you asked for help from the right person? Find someone who has done what you are trying to do and ask them for suggestions and support. They should be able to help you create a plan specific to your needs and goals.

G

As we express our gratitude,
we must never forget
that the highest appreciation
is not to utter words
but to live by them.
~ John F. Kennedy

G – Gratitude

When was the last time you told someone how grateful you were for their love and support or just being a positive influence in your life? How did you show your appreciation? Was it verbal, written, in-person, a phone call, video, or text message? How did it make you feel, and how did the person react?

Expressing gratitude is an easy way to shift your mindset from negative and self-defeating to positive and appreciative. Studies have shown that expressions of gratitude have psychological, social, and physical benefits that promote overall health. Expressing gratitude also enhances empathy, reduces stress, lowers depression, and improves self-esteem and happiness.

Set aside time daily to acknowledge the people, places, and things that we often take for granted, like food, clothes, shelter, family, friends, and freedom. It only takes a few moments a day to pause and reflect on the goodness in our lives, no matter our circumstances.

Dr. Gwen's Self-Care Tip:

Here are three gratitude exercises that you can try.

1. Gratitude Journal

Every day, spend a few minutes writing down things you are grateful for that happened during the day. Small things count too! Examples could be receiving a compliment, hearing from a friend or family member, eating a favorite meal, or learning a new skill. The key is to be consistent. Make gratitude journaling a part of your daily self-care routine.

2. Write a Gratitude Letter or Thank You Note

Showing appreciation for someone who has been there for you in your time of need in kind words or deeds is a great way to express gratitude. Think of someone who has helped you in some way (big or small) that positively impacted your life. This person could be a family member, friend, colleague, community member, etc. Write a letter that explains what you appreciate about them and why. It helps to include specific examples and details regarding how their kindness helped you. The letter doesn't have to be long. In fact, you might just want to start with a thank you note, as long as it's written with sincere gratitude. You may choose to hold on to the letter in remembrance and as a reminder that you are not alone, throw it away or share it with the person. It's up to you. The important thing is acknowledgment.

Here are some ways to start.

Say:

I can't thank you enough for...

It really helped me out when you...

Thank you for being there when....

3. Verbal Expressions

Saying thank you, I appreciate you, or I'm sorry can be one of the simplest, most direct ways to express gratitude to the people you hold in high esteem or those you may have taken for granted. Expressing your feelings after some reflection is a great way to show appreciation and mend broken relationships. It's never too late to say I'm sorry or give thanks. Dropping by for a visit, scheduling a lunch or dinner date, or simply picking up the phone for a heart-to-heart conversation are effective ways to communicate your appreciation for someone special.

Gratitude Flower

Think about the people, places, things, and events you are grateful for and place them on a petal. Then, when you are feeling down, look at your flower and reflect on all the things that make you feel happy, loved, and appreciated.

H

Cleanliness is the first law of health.

H – Hygiene

Good personal hygiene has personal and social benefits. However, hygiene is one of the first things to go when the going gets tough. As an educator (teacher and counselor), poor hygiene was a blaring red flag that there might be problems that require support. For example, a lot of people struggle to do basic hygiene tasks when depressed or they have low self-esteem. I found this true during my tenure, especially with teenagers and boys. Hygiene can include bathing, washing their hands, brushing their teeth, combing their hair, or wearing clean clothes. So, check in with yourself: have you combed your hair, showered, or done laundry this week? It's important for your physical and mental health.

Dr. Gwen's Self-Care Tip:

Daily Hygiene

1

*Be addicted
to constant
and never-ending
self-improvement.*

~ Anthony J. D'Angelo

I – Improvements

There is always something about us we can improve. We are all works in progress with limitless potential. Making improvements in your life is important to being there for yourself and others. Don't focus so much on who you used to be. Focus on who you are BECOMING. Focus on who you CHOOSE to be.

As a passionate self-care enthusiast, growth advocate, and counselor, I'm constantly looking for ways to self-improve. Throughout this book, I've provided practical information and guided you through self-improvement activities to help you get on track and stay on track. In fact, this entire book was written with self-improvement in mind. It will be helpful for you to **set personal and professional goals** that you want to achieve. You can do this by simply creating a list of short and long-term goals, or you can flex your creative muscle as you make your vision board.

As you work on self-improvement, surround yourself with a tribe of people who match your energy and use that energy to create the life you desire, to grow, and to heal. I call these people my uplifters, encouragers, supporters, cheerleaders, prayer warriors, bucket fillers, and accountability partners. I read somewhere that you are the sum of the three to five people you spend the most time with. Ask yourself if the people you spend the most time with are helping or hindering you from reaching your goals. Do these people want the best for you and your life? Their energy, attitude, and habits should align with who you are but, more importantly, who you are becoming.

Dr. Gwen's Self-Care Tip:

What is a goal you want to achieve?

Now write down the three to five people you regularly spend the most time with. **Then, write the value each of these people brings to your life**. For example, supporter, prayer warrior, cheerleader, etc. If you can't find positive things to say about the people you spend the most time with or see the value they bring, you probably need to find a new tribe.

1.

2.

3.

4.

5.

J

Journaling increases your self-confidence. It helps you look at how far you've come and how you overcame previous seemingly impossible obstacles.

~ Jeremiah Say

J – Journal (Gratitude, Reflection, Mood, Drawing).

Journaling is a way to write down your thoughts and feelings to understand them better. If you're like too many of us, journaling is a fleeting thought. If you happen to be one of the people who own a journal, it is more than likely tucked away on a shelf or in a drawer that you occasionally open. Maybe you've been intimidated by the thought of writing or, better yet, knowing what to write. Let me put your mind at ease and provide some motivation to get started.

There are countless studies that show journaling as a powerful way to boost your mental health, reduce depression and anxiety, and make you an all-around happier person. There are many types of journals to choose from: gratitude, reflection, mood, drawing, affirmations, poetry, and the list goes on and on. Some people prefer to keep multiple journals, while others prefer keeping all their thoughts in one place. Do what works best for you. The journal you're most likely to use regularly is what I recommend.

How to journal: Try these tips to help you get started.

1. **Write daily.** Set aside a few minutes to routinely write every day—for example, first thing in the morning or at bedtime.

2. **Make it convenient.** Keep your journal and a pen in plain sight. It will serve as a visual reminder that you have everything you need when it's time to write.

3. **Keep it simple.** You don't have to write your deepest darkest secrets or be sophisticated. Journaling is your own private space to reflect and express your thoughts and feelings. Let your mind wander, and your words and ideas flow freely. Don't worry about spelling mistakes or what other people might think. The journal is for you by you.

Keeping a journal helps you be in control when it seems like your world is a mess. Journaling is a great way to solve problems when you are stressed, frustrated, or overwhelmed. Start by identifying the source of your stress, then create a plan to minimize or resolve the cause of your stress. Journaling is a healthy way to express yourself. You get to know yourself by sharing your most private fears, thoughts, feelings, hopes, and dreams. Look at your writing time as personal "me time." It is a time when you can de-stress, wind down and clear your mind. Journaling should be a time you look forward to doing something to improve your mind, body, and soul.

Dr. Gwen's Self-Care Tip:

Here are a few prompts to get your journal writing started. I recommend picking up the *Free Your Mind: Rise, Reflect Reform Journal*. It is a combination of many of the journals I reference above and may help you determine which kind works best for you.

Who is your biggest supporter? Why?

Where is your dream vacation destination? Why?

What is the hardest thing you've ever had to do? Why?

How do you feel at this very moment? Why?

What is your proudest accomplishment? Why?

What is something you are looking forward to doing? Why?

K

Keep your head up

and stay strong.

Make them wonder

how you're still standing

and smiling.

K – Keep Your Head Up

Life is full of ups and downs. One minute we may be on top of the world, and the next, seemingly in the depths of hell. One thing we can all agree on is during those times of despair, we should keep a positive attitude and outlook, embrace the need for change, and be open to new growth opportunities. I'm not suggesting you shouldn't allow yourself to feel your feelings. Crying is actually very cathartic, so open the floodgates if you need to release your emotions. However, don't stay in that space too long. I have a saying that helps me on those days when I'm in my feelings that I'd like to share with you. **I tell myself that today I can be pitiful, but tomorrow I have to be powerful again.**

So much of taking care of yourself is being aware of what your needs are and ensuring that your needs are met. Make a conscious effort to observe yourself during challenging times— your moods, thoughts, behavior patterns, triggers, and your vulnerabilities. Journaling is a great way to gather this information while tracking your growth and progress. Sometimes it may seem as if we are stuck because we are looking at the end goal instead of paying attention to our growth over time.

Here are a few ways to keep your head up and a smile on your face during those tough times:

1. **Express gratitude**: Refer to letter G, where we discussed the benefits of expressions of gratitude.

2. **Look for the silver lining**: No matter what you are going through, look for the growth opportunity. It's what I call the blessing in the lesson.

3. **Lean into your support system**: Use your family and friends for support. Don't be too proud to ask for help. You are the only one who knows what support you need to elevate out of your current situation.

4. **Spend time being one with nature**: Anyone following me has inevitably heard about my garden, which I refer to as my happy place. There's something about being in nature that gives you a boost and improves your mood.

5. **Random Acts of Kindness**: Being kind doesn't cost a thing and can instantly brighten someone's day. In turn, it will brighten yours too. The good feelings that come from helping others are linked to emotional well-being.

Dr. Gwen's Self-Care Tip:

Sometimes all we need is a little distraction to take our mind off what's bringing us down. I'm not trying to minimize or make light of your current situation or circumstance. I'm simply trying to allow you a moment for your brain to breathe and take a break from the stress.

Try this simple brain teaser activity.

How many words can you create from the slogan **KEEP YOUR HEAD UP**? Each letter can only be used the number of times it appears in the slogan. So, for example, there's only one K but three E's. Here are three words to get you started.

1. read
2. heard
3. ready

L

I've learned

that I still have

a lot to learn.

~ Maya Angelou

L – Learn a New Skill or Hobby.

Are you wasting your life away scrolling on social media? Are you bored? Do you have extra time on your hands? Are you trying to find your life's purpose? Are you feeling stuck? Having a hobby is a great way to spend your spare time and unwind from your daily routine - whether it's learning a new skill, doing something outdoors, reading, or doing something musical or artistic. Hobbies provide you with a sense of accomplishment, teach you about your strengths and talents, and provide opportunities to meet new people with shared interests. Learning a new skill is a chance to step outside your comfort zone and do something you have always wanted to do.

Participating in a hobby may be the mental and physical boost you need. Spending time on enjoyable activities can improve your mental health, confidence, and well-being. Research shows that people with hobbies are less likely to suffer from stress, low mood, and depression. Learning a new skill can also improve your confidence and overall sense of well-being. Although learning a new skill can be challenging, embracing new growth opportunities is important. You don't have to be perfect or even good at the skill; just be open and receptive, embrace the experience, and have fun.

Activities that get you out and about can make you feel happier and more relaxed. Group activities like team sports can improve your communication skills and relationships with others. Your interests may be creative, athletic, academic, or personal. You may choose a hobby you can do alone or as part of a group. Whatever your interests are, there is sure to be a hobby out there for you. What matters is that it is something you find meaningful and enjoyable.

Hobbies can range from being a romance novel junkie like myself to participating in or attending sporting events. Regardless of your hobby, it can greatly benefit your mind, body, social life, and even your career. Of course, the benefits of each hobby will differ depending on how much time, energy, and passion you devote to it. Nevertheless, hobbies can have benefits that can help you in the short and long term.

Here are some things for you to consider as you explore potential hobbies.

1. What are your interests in life?

2. What activities do you enjoy doing alone or in a group?

3. What activities fit your time, schedule, and lifestyle?

4. Write down five skills or hobbies you will try because you see value, purpose, and benefits.

   1.

   2.

   3.

   4.

   5.

Dr. Gwen's Self-Care Tip:

Here are 20 ideas to get you started. What are you passionate about? There is something here for everyone. People are learning new skills on the internet, for free, daily! Learning a new skill or hobby can be a fun stress relieving activity, side hustle, way to stay in shape, and keep your creative juices flowing.

It is never

too late to

LEARN

something new.

YOU CAN DO IT!

Building
Sports
Cooking/Baking
Welding
Mechanics
Teaching
Acting/Performing
Being in Nature
Reading
Heating/Air
Arts & Crafts
Volunteering
Documentaries
Photography
Painting
DIY Projects
Decorating
Jewelry Making
Cosmetology
Music

M

A mentor is someone who allows you to see the hope inside you.

~ Oprah Winfrey

M – Mentor

Find a successful family member, friend, or community leader who inspires you. If possible, ask this person if they are willing to share their experiences (positive and negative), skills, training, career path, opinions, and suggestions about how they achieved success with you. Most people will be more than willing to lend a helping hand to a RISING, resilient star like YOU. Having a mentor can significantly broaden your career and life goals and opportunities.

Dr. Gwen's Self-Care Tip

Refer back to the list of people who you can ask for help and call on for support in letter A. Remember, asking for help is one of the most courageous moves you can make when starting over. It means you won't have to face challenges alone, no matter how big or small they may seem. It helps the load feel lighter when you know that there are people in your corner that you can call on when you need help,

Here are a few ways a mentor can support you. However, mentoring should be a two-way street. So, think of ways to give back and provide value to your mentor. What skills do you bring to the table?

- Resume writing
- SMART goals (specific, measurable, attainable, realistic, timebound)

- Roleplaying
- Networking
- Job shadowing
- Job interviews
- Professional groups
- Volunteer opportunities
- Conferences/Workshops
- Resources (videos, podcasts, templates, etc.)
- Internships
- Vision and mission statements
- References
- Financial literacy
- Business development
- Sounding board
- Work/life balance
- Leadership skills

> Mentorship is a brain to pick,
> an ear to listen,
> and a push in the right direction.
>
> ~John C. Crosby

N

At the end of the day, let there be

no excuses,

no explanations,

no regrets.

— Dr. Steve Maraboli

N – No Excuses

We do not always accept failure, take responsibility for our actions, or accept that we made a mistake with grace. Making excuses may start out innocently; after all, who likes failure or defeat and the resulting consequences? However, making excuses may quickly become a way to avoid responsibilities or undesirable tasks. **You can quickly develop a habit of blaming others or circumstances for your shortcomings.** For example, I'll never make it, I can't catch a break, I don't have time, I don't have enough education, nobody will help me, I don't have a car, I can't break this habit…and the list goes on and on.

I know some of you are filled with self-doubt, and you are easily intimidated by the skills, popularity, or success of others. You may lack confidence and struggle with self-esteem, especially if you have a mental or physical disability. **But I'm here to tell you that YOU are stronger than your strongest excuse and DESERVE everything you secretly desire.** Don't keep doing the same things and expecting different results. That is the definition of insanity. Life just doesn't work that way. The real world won't accept excuses for your behavior. Your spouse/mate won't accept your excuses (at least they shouldn't), your friends won't accept them, your boss won't accept them, and the legal system won't accept them. Stop making excuses.

Focus your energy on your goals, not the obstacles, and start making changes and decisions that elevate you to the next level instead of blaming others for why you are not where you want to be in life.

I'm not suggesting that the solution to your problems is a quick fix or easy to find. However, the solution is out there if you are ready to find it and not afraid of stepping outside your comfort zone. In most cases, you know what you need to do. Stop procrastinating and making excuses. Like the Nike slogan says, "Just Do It." Remember, don't be afraid or too proud to ask for help.

Taking responsibility for your actions and seeking solutions to problems are critical components as you start over and begin anew. Capitalize on the opportunities that come your way.

Dr. Gwen's Self-Care Tip:

Excuses keep you from progressing and accomplishing your goals. Here are some things you can do instead of making excuses.

STOP making EXCUSES

Exhausted?	Rest
Out of Shape?	Get Moving
No Time?	Limit Social Media
Overwhelmed?	Simplify
Don't Know?	Ask Somebody

O

*Apologize for
your mistakes,
your behavior,
or your attitude,
NOT your feelings.*

O – Own Your Mistakes

We all make mistakes, struggle, encounter challenges, and deal with the resulting consequences. Mistakes are a part of the learning and growth process of life. Unfortunately, a lot of people won't admit when they are wrong or when they make a mistake. Chalk it up to ego, pride, ignorance, or just being set in their ways. However, one of the best things you can do is admit when you are wrong, sincerely apologize, ask for forgiveness from the people impacted, and move on. PLEASE don't rationalize or follow your apology with an excuse or reason for not "doing *the right thing*." That's not the way to learn from your mistakes. It also doesn't show accountability or integrity, which are needed to earn the respect and trust of others.

Self-improvement entails owning and taking responsibility for your mistakes, learning from them, and doing better in the future. When you know better, DO better. Don't let past mistakes hinder your growth and progress. **You ARE NOT the sum of your mistakes.** They do not define you. Let me say that again. You ARE NOT the sum of your mistakes.

What is the biggest mistake you have ever made?

What lesson did you learn?

How did you overcome it?

Dr. Gwen's Self-Care Tip:

- Don't let a little mistake turn into a big problem by rationalizing or justifying it.

- The sooner you own up to your mistake, the sooner you can move past it.

- Owning your mistakes will improve your problem-solving skills.

- Surround yourself with people who give you honest feedback and hold you accountable for your actions. These people tell you what you need to hear instead of what you want to hear. Essentially, these are the people in your tribe who want to see you grow and thrive.

P

It's the
REPETITION
of affirmations that leads to
BELIEF.
And once that belief
becomes a deep
CONVICTION,
things begin to happen.

~ Muhammad Ali

P – Positive Affirmations

What are affirmations? I'm so glad you asked. Positive affirmations are phrases, quotes, or, simply put, positive statements you say to yourself. Affirmations are a helpful way to minimize those overwhelming negative, self-defeating, self-sabotaging thoughts that are often on constant replay in your mind. We all deal with what we call imposter syndrome. Let me break it down for you. You know those negative, unhealthy, self-sabotaging thoughts we tell ourselves that keep us stuck. Our bodies and minds often latch on to insecurities, pain, and hate associated with traumatic experiences. Consequently, here are a few examples of negative messages we tell ourselves:

1. I'm not good enough.

2. I can't do this.

3. I'll never amount to anything.

4. I don't deserve to be happy.

5. He/She is better off without me.

When these negative thoughts enter your mind, stop giving them energy by listening to them. If you focus on negative thoughts that cross your mind, then that'swhat you will start believing. So instead, try shifting your mindset and current way of thinking by training your brain to focus on the good and bring more positive light into your life.

Negative thoughts are often a reaction to the trauma, pain, and guilt we carry associated with past experiences. By practicing positive affirmations, you are reforming your way of thinking, which can lead to healing from the past. Positive affirmations are personal and should be statements that reflect your insecurities, experiences, desires, and dreams. Find which ones work best for you and use them daily.

In addition to minimizing negative thoughts, studies have found that using affirmations decreases stress, increases motivation, improves overall mood and happiness levels, and boosts self-esteem and self-worth. Positive affirmations can change the way you feel about yourself, thereby altering your attitude, mindset, behaviors, and ultimately your life. You can achieve great things.

Dr. Gwen's Self-Care Tip:

Here are three ways to use affirmations in your daily life.

1. Create your own affirmations or find ones that speak to you based on your needs and what will help you the most. Don't just recite generic affirmations that don't align with your overall goals.

2. Be consistent. Try repeating your affirmations at the same time each day and repeating them several times. For example, say them five times each morning or night while brushing your teeth.

3. Be patient and give yourself some grace. Change doesn't happen overnight. It may take some time before you see changes in your overall mood, but that doesn't mean that your hard work and commitment aren't making a difference.

Below are examples of affirmations to get you started improving your daily thoughts.
- I am resilient.
- I am not limited by what others think of me.
- I am blessed with a supportive family.
- I am planning for success.
- I am releasing fear and doubt.

Now it's time for you to write some affirmations of your own.

1.

2.

3.

4.

5.

The secret to breaking any bad habit is to love something greater than the habit.

— Bryant McGill

Q – Quit Bad Habits

We all have bad habits, such as overeating, poor work/life balance, not exercising, drinking too much, and so on, and so forth. Unfortunately, these bad habits can have a negative impact not only on our health (physical and mental) but on our finances and relationships.

This book is about new beginnings. So, it's time for a change. Now is the time to stop making excuses and living with your bad habits. Remember, insanity is doing the same thing repeatedly and expecting a different result. So, let's take the time to evaluate what isn't working for you on your journey to becoming your best self and start making the necessary changes.

Change might not be fast, and it won't be easy in most cases. However, with time and consistent effort, almost any bad habit can be stopped. There are many habits we know are bad for us, like drinking and driving, while there may be others that we haven't considered, like staying in an unhealthy relationship, not taking brain breaks, or multitasking.

Here are 10 Bad habits to STOP.

1. Procrastination
2. Poor sleep hygiene
3. Eating unhealthily
4. Nail biting
5. Substance abuse
6. Too much social media
7. Being a couch potato
8. Negative self-talk
9. Overspending
10. Lying

Can you name five more bad habits?

1.

2.

3.

4.

5.

What bad habit do you need to quit immediately to make your life more positive, healthier, and happier?

How will your life change when you quit this bad habit?

Dr. Gwen's Self-Care Tip

Here are five ways to break bad habits.

1. Replace a bad habit with a good one.

2. Start with small changes.

3. Recruit a trusted friend or family member for accountability and support.

4. Prepare for roadblocks and challenges that might tempt you to revert to old habits.

5. Celebrate your big and small wins.

R

A person who won't read has no advantage over a person who can't read.

— *Mark Twain*

R – Read Books

There are many benefits to reading. Allowing myself to get lost in a mindless romance novel is often my great escape from the worries and challenges of a stressful day. A 2009 study at the University of Sussex showed that stress is reduced by 68% just by reading! So, the next time you feel stressed, grab a book, lose yourself in the storylines, and allow your mind and body to relax.

Of course, I don't just read for pleasure. I read for success, knowledge, and self-improvement. You can literally learn anything from reading a book. I know what some of you smarty pants out there are thinking…I Google it, or I can get that information from YouTube. I agree to a certain extent. However, read a book if you want to learn about something in depth from a scholarly professional with years of experience and not just someone like a YouTuber interested in the topic trying to gain followers. Trust me; you will absorb and retain more information. If you are like me, you will highlight, tab, or underline important information that you can quickly go back and reference.

So, what are you interested in learning?

Perhaps you want to learn how to fix or build something, become a vegetarian, gain leadership skills, or start a business. Maybe you want to learn how to "say no" without feeling guilty. Or perhaps you want to figure out how to start over after divorce, incarnation, or relocating?

Whatever information you seek, you can find it by reading a book.

Dr. Gwen's Self-Care Tip:

Don't let word of mouth, social media posts, text messages, and news headlines be your only source of information. Here are twelve benefits of reading to encourage you to pick up a book.

1. Reduces stress and helps you relax
2. Improves your focus, concentration, and memory
3. Builds vocabulary and understanding
4. Improves self-confidence
5. Enhances your knowledge
6. Increases your imagination and creativity
7. Improves your communication skills
8. Entertainment
9. Increases academic performance
10. Increases understanding of other cultures
11. Exercises your brain
12. Improves your ability to empathize

What is the last book that you read?

Did you read it for pleasure, information, self-improvement, or education?

Would you recommend it to others? Why or why not?

S

Surround yourself by people who are going to lift you higher.

— Oprah Winfrey

S – Stay Connected

Staying connected, especially in an increasingly isolated world, is more important than ever. Staying connected means being present with people, literally and figuratively speaking. For example, feeling seen, heard, and understood by others. In essence, staying connected is as much a state of mind as a state of being. **Sometimes the connection is a heart-to-heart, ugly cry, get-it-all-out long overdue talk. But sometimes, it's just a laugh-out-loud text or e-mail that comes at just the right time.** Reach out to your friends, family, coworkers, and community members who can provide emotional support and practical help. You don't have to be alone.

People who are not socially connected are more vulnerable to anxiety, depression, antisocial behavior, and even suicidal behaviors, further increasing their isolation. One study found that lack of social connection is a more significant determinant of health than obesity, smoking, and high blood pressure. In contrast, strong social connection leads to a 50% increased chance of longevity. Other studies have found that people who feel more connected have

- Lower rates of anxiety and depression
- Higher self-esteem
- More empathy

- More trust

- Better cooperation

- Increased happiness

Dr. Gwen's Self-Care Tip:

This year I opened a private counseling practice after working in schools for over twenty-five years. I went from never having a few moments of solitude during the workday (if I was lucky and planned it with fidelity) to being in a big office by myself all day. Although I am very passionate about my job and love what I do, I must admit being alone in the office all day was a bit lonely at times. As a result, I started looking for ways to stay connected with others personally and professionally for my own mental health. For example, I started scheduling lunch dates with my husband a few days a week instead of eating alone in the office. I also started looking at the events calendars of different organizations where I was a member and scheduling events I was interested in attending on my calendar. Attending community events provides opportunities to network and form collaborative partnerships.

Here are some things to consider as you start connecting with others.

- Don't be shy. Say hello and introduce yourself!

- What are your interests or hobbies?

- What kind of personalities are you naturally comfortable around?

- How can you get involved in your community?
- Join a club, social, or professional organization.
- Volunteer.
- Mix and mingle with colleagues at work.
- Create opportunities to spend time with family and friends.
- Step outside your comfort zone.
- Attend community networking events.
- Enroll in a class or attend a workshop that interests you.

What other ways do you stay connected or plan to start making connections?

1.

2.

3.

4.

5.

T

There is no greater agony than bearing an untold story inside you.

– Maya Angelou

T – Try Therapy

Have you considered going to therapy but are still on the fence and haven't taken action to get started? You are not alone. Seeking help from a mental health professional is one of those decisions that many people grapple over. Sometimes, the fear of the unknown or common misconceptions about therapy deters people from getting the help they desperately need. Unfortunately, not all of us are lucky enough to have trusted friends or colleagues who can listen and give us good, sound advice. That's when a therapist can come in handy.

10 Reasons You Should Try Therapy

1. You have unhealthy coping strategies such as drug use.

2. You are grieving the loss of a loved one.

3. You are having family problems.

4. You suspect you have a mental health condition.

5. You need to talk to someone other than your friends and family, or you have no one to talk to about your problems.

6. You are someone with a terminal illness or the caregiver of someone with a terminal illness.

7. You have a mental health disorder.

8. You feel overwhelmingly sad and hopeless.

9. You are dealing with or considering a significant life change such as divorce, relocation, or career.

10. You have trouble appropriately managing emotions such as anger, frustration, disappointment, etc.

Dr. Gwen's Self-Care Tip:

Still on the fence. Here are some of the benefits of therapy that may finally encourage you to get the help you need. Allowing yourself space and time to focus on YOUrself is one of the most compassionate things you can do to take care of YOU.

Benefits of Therapy

- Help improve communication and interpersonal skills
- Learn to make healthier choices
- Develop coping strategies
- Change self-defeating thoughts, behaviors, and habits
- Acquire problem-solving and conflict-resolution skills
- Get relief from depression, anxiety, and other mental health conditions
- Practice self-reflection and awareness, and feel empowered

U

Unplug

and

reconnect with

yourself and others.

U – Unplug

Are you spending too much time on social media? Are you over-reliant on social media platforms such as Facebook, Twitter, Snapchat, YouTube, and Instagram for information and connections with others? Is your relationship with technology impacting your ability to foster face-to-face interactions and healthy relationships? Tell the truth! If you spend excessive amounts of time plugged into technology, literally and figuratively, and are experiencing feelings of sadness, dissatisfaction, frustration, or loneliness, it may be time to unplug and reset.

I know you don't want to miss out on anything, and you have a front-row seat to people **seemingly** "living their best life" every day on social media. But stop and think for a minute. Does the thought of EVERYONE but you having the best marriage/mate, an endless number of friends, taking lavish vacations, receiving promotions, etc., fill you with infinite joy or overwhelming feelings of jealousy, inadequacy, and sadness? Feeling others are happier and having more fun than you through these "snapshots" of their lives can wreak havoc on your emotional and mental health. The HERE and NOW will help you live a more well-balanced life by limiting social media and focusing on your life in REAL time.

When you spend too much time plugged into technology, especially social media, whether it's your phone, iPad, computer, tv, gaming, etc., you may neglect your responsibilities to yourself, loved ones, home, school, or work. Here are some other negative impacts of too much technology.

1. Social learning deficits
2. Sleep problems
3. Isolation/Loneliness
4. Anxiety and depression
5. Self-harm
6. Suicidal thoughts
7. Addiction

Dr. Gwen's Self-Care Tip:

Here are five ways to unplug and reduce screen time.

1. Use an app to track how much time you spend on social media each day. Then set a goal to reduce the time.
2. Turn off your phone at certain times of the day, such as when driving, during meals, while in the presence of others, and at bedtime.
3. Disable social media notifications to minimize being distracted and overwhelmed by the constant buzzing, beeping, chirping, and dinging of your phone.

4. Remove social media apps from your phone, so you can only check Facebook, Twitter, and the like from your tablet or computer.

5. Pledge to not turn your phone on each morning for a set amount of time. For example, the first 30 minutes after waking up.

You've heard of plug and play.

This is plug, unplug, and play.

It's so simple to use,

it's unbelievable.

~ Steve Jobs

V

Where there is no

VISION

there is no

HOPE.

— *George Washington Carver*

V – Vision Boards

Visualization is a way to manifest your goals and dreams. It is **the practice of imagining what you want to achieve in the future**. However, you act as if what you visualize were true today. In essence, you begin with the end in mind. Goal setting is important at every age and stage in your life. Creating a vision board can help you lay out your ideal future using pictures (draw, cut, and paste), words (affirmations, quotes, phrases, slogans, graffiti), and emotions (joy, relief, peace). Vision boards allow you to stop, think, and plan where you want to BE in the future, physically, psychologically, emotionally, spiritually, and professionally. It involves engaging all five senses of sight, smell, touch, taste, and hearing to imagine what your life would be like if you manifest your dreams. Visuals help to make your goals and dreams more tangible and concrete. Visual imagery will increase your motivation and determination while serving as a reminder of the life you dream of living. However, a vision board is only as beneficial as the work you are willing to do. Be creative and let your imagination run free as you make your vision board as thorough, exciting, and detailed as possible. Dream BIG!

What If Your Vision Board Came True?

You Are What You Manifest!

Benefits of Vision Boards

One of the most powerful benefits of a vision board is that it builds confidence, solidifies your dreams, and turns thoughts into possibilities. No matter what you believe about yourself or how much fear and self-doubt you have, a vision board completed with fidelity will slowly transform your self-defeating thoughts, behaviors, and beliefs into a more confident, self-motivated, and growth mindset. It is okay if you start with vague self-care goals. The important thing is that you START. Then, you can clarify and fine-tune your goals as you go and grow.

Vision board should be placed somewhere that you visit often to help you stay motivated. Every time you look at it, you will be reminded of your goal – whether that is to graduate, travel, learn a new skill, reduce or eliminate debt, get healthy, adhere to boundaries, or get more sleep. Our lives are constantly changing, so you should be able to check images and goals off the board as they are accomplished and add new ones in their place. When you reflect on and evaluate your progression, seeing how much you have accomplished will be a source of pride in knowing you did something for YOU. Achieving your goals will not only make you feel good, but it will also help you find your life's purpose. It is okay to think outside the box and color outside the lines.

Dr. Gwen's Self-Care Tip:

Here are some tips for creating your vision board:

1. **Schedule Time to Create It** – Take time to focus on YOU. Light a candle, turn on some soft music and let the visualization begin. Creating a vision board should be a fun time spent getting in touch with your innermost thoughts, hopes, and dreams.

2. **Ask: What Makes YOU Most Happy?** – "Happy" means something different to everybody. Think of the people, places, and things that make you happiest, and find ways to incorporate more of that positive energy into your life.

3. **Find Visual Representations** – find images and words (in magazines or online) that relate to the dreams and goals you expressed above.

4. **Make a Collage** – Use the space provided on the next page to draw (art, doodle, symbols, stick figures) or stick various items, such as photographs, quotes, affirmations, magazine clippings, etc., to depict your ideal future.

Sample Vision Board

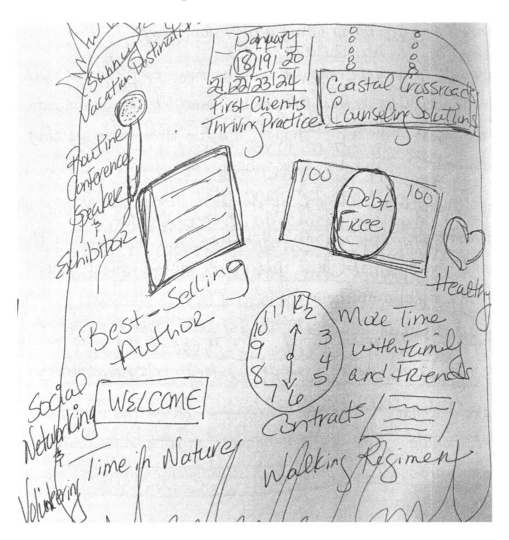

Sample Vision Board

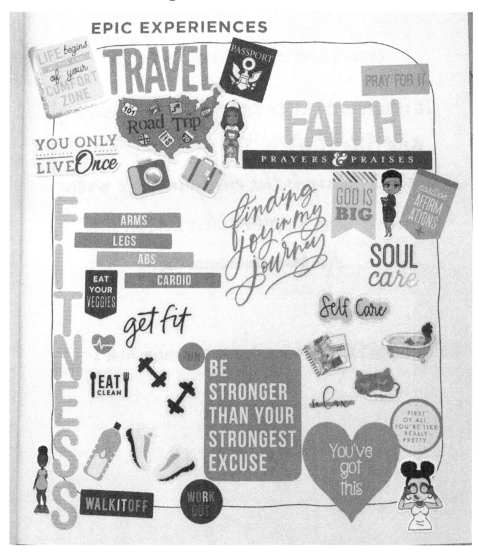

Create a Vision Board

W

Writing is the best way to talk without being interrupted.

— Jules Renard

W – Write (Letters, Songs, Poetry)

Writing is an effective way to reflect on difficult times in your life and create some space to heal. Change and healing begin when you start appreciating your life experiences, even the unpleasant and painful ones, and see how they have led you to be who you are today and who you can be in the future. We all have gone through difficult things in our lives that have impacted us in major ways. Although we can't go back in time and change things (wouldn't that be nice), we can reflect and acknowledge the fact that we made it through those difficult times. Writing about your past experiences, hopes, and dreams will help remind you that you are worthy of everything you desire and have everything you need to make it happen.

A great place to start is by writing a letter to your younger self. In this letter, reflect on how far you have come. Tell what you have learned over the years that gives you strength, courage, and resilience during difficult times. Be open and honest with yourself while sharing specific lessons or topics you wish your younger self had known that could have prevented some heartache and pain. You can keep this letter and your learnings to yourself. If you feel comfortable doing so, you can share the experience and what you have learned with someone you trust. In difficult situations, read this letter to yourself as a reminder that you are strong and resilient! Keep rising!

You may also choose to write letters to people you care about, who care about you, and who support you. This might be a letter to parents, a friend, a mentor, or simply someone who helped you along the way. In the letters, you can say what you wish you had known, what you wish you had said, what you want to say one day, or take the opportunity to express gratitude for how they helped you. You can choose to send these letters, keep them, or throw them away.

Dr. Gwen's Self-Care Tip:

Here is a list of questions and prompts to guide you as you write.

1. What is a difficult situation you overcame?
2. What is the significance of this situation?
3. How did you feel during this time?
4. How did you react at the time?
5. What, if anything, did you do to take care of yourself?
6. What do you wish you could have said or done differently?
7. Are there beliefs you developed about yourself or your life because of this situation?
8. What wisdom, support, knowledge, or care do you wish someone would have given you during this difficult time?
9. What lessons did you learn?
10. How will you communicate your needs from now on?

Tough times don't last, but talents and gifts do.

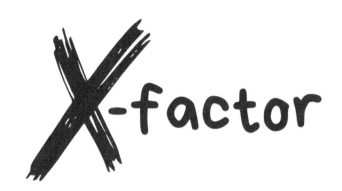

X – X-factor

I guess you are wondering what an x-factor is and how it's going to help you. In this instance, I've chosen to use the x-factor as another way of saying your "superpower." In essence, it is the strengths and talents you possess that make you unique and set you apart from others. You may have heard the term used in games or talent shows.

My superpower is teaching. As I've been known to say, some people "are **called** to teach" (like preaching), and some "**stumble** into teaching"! I am blessed to be among those with the innate ability to teach. I'm a damn good teacher if I do say so myself. Yes, I'm tooting my own horn. I'm very passionate about teaching and helping others, especially children, which is evident in how they respond to me.

I believe we all have x-factors. However, many of us are not utilizing our superpowers or haven't yet discovered or honed in on our hidden talents. Discovering your x-factor may require a mentor or coach, as discussed in letter M. It may involve learning a new skill or hobby and opening your mind to new growth opportunities. Refer to letter L. Volunteering may be another way to unleash your superpower. Once you discover your x-factor, use it to its fullest potential to elevate, increase your chances of success, and manifest your dreams.

Dr. Gwen's Self-Care Tip:

1. **Ask family, friends, and colleagues what they admire about you.**

   During a virtual birthday party at the height of the pandemic, I asked a group of close friends to share one word to describe me. I wrote down their responses so I could reflect on them later. I found many themes and patterns in their responses. Lucky for me, most of what they said is representative of my life's work and authentic to who I am at my core. Having said that, I do have some superpowers that I don't particularly like to use, and that's okay. I am happy just knowing that others see them as a strength.

2. **Make a Strengths List**

   A strengths list simply entails listing all the things you do well. Make sure you enjoy it if you plan to use it to elevate your life. Look for patterns in what you're good at, including skills and character traits.

3. **Write down your proudest accomplishments.**

   Make a list of your top five to ten proudest accomplishments. These accomplishments could be anything that you deem an achievement. For example, although earning my doctorate is a major accomplishment, working through the challenges of a twenty-plus-year marriage is too. The goal is to write victories, big or small, that are most meaningful to you. Then, reflect on the skills, strengths, and talents you used to overcome challenges and persevere to reach goals and achieve each accomplishment.

Y

SAY

YES!

Y – YES

Just like you should say no to things you don't really want to do, you should say yes to the things that align with your overall goals and the vision you have of yourself in the future. Don't let fear and self-doubt keep you from manifesting your dreams. Say YES to new adventures and learning opportunities. Take calculated risks.

Say YES to:

- taking some "ME time." Your needs matter too!
- starting that night class. It's a learning and growth opportunity.
- going to that party where you only know the host. Expand your social circle.
- applying for that promotion. You are qualified.
- going on a date. Don't turn down a free meal.
- letting others help you. There's no need to suffer in silence.
- having that piece of cake. You deserve it! Moderation is the key.
- spontaneous events. Live a little. Okay, a lot!
- Volunteering. You may discover a new passion, and it's a great way to network and learn new things.

Dr. Gwen's Self-Care Tip:

Complete that vision board. Yeah, I know some of you skipped right over that part. Remember, I said creating your vision board is a great way to build confidence, solidify your dreams, and turn your thoughts into possibilities. So what are you waiting for? Get that vision board completed. Make sure it reflects the outcome of some of those YESes.

If your vision board is complete, good for you; **WAY TO GO!** Do something to reward yourself for staying on track. Celebrate this small win.

Z

Worry Less

SLEEP

More!

Z – Zzzzzzs

Do you have trouble falling asleep, staying asleep, or sleeping too much or too little? Do you struggle to get out of bed in the mornings? What about struggling to stay awake during the day? Well, you are not alone. Many people complain of being tired and sleepy all the time.

Scientific research shows that many of us do not get enough sleep. You need 7-8 hours of sleep every night to be at your best. While work, social obligations, extra-curricular activities, family time, and chores make it seemingly impossible to get the recommended amount of sleep, it's important to try to get as much as possible. Lack of sleep can significantly impact your physical, mental, and emotional health, resulting in fatigue and unhappiness or depression and anxiety. On the flip side, a good night's sleep can give you the energy and clarity you need just to get through the day.

Although getting enough sleep may not seem like a big deal, a report from the National Sleep Foundation breaks the amount of sleep that adults need into age-specific ranges with allowances for personal preferences. For example, they recommend

- Adults, 65+ years: 7 to 8 hours.
- Adults, 26 to 64 years: 7 to 9 hours.
- Young adults, 18 to 25 years: 7 to 9 hours.

If you are not getting proper sleep and giving your body a chance to rest and recharge daily, you may

- Increase your chances of health problems such as heart attacks, diabetes, strokes, etc.
- have trouble with focus and attention.
- lack motivation to complete tasks.
- have more car accidents.
- engage in risky behavior (drugs and alcohol, sex, violence).
- experience anxiety and depression.

Dr. Gwen's Self-Care Tip:

Here are a few suggestions to help you get adequate sleep:

- Go to bed at a consistent time every night.
- Sleep in your bed instead of on the couch.
- Exercise daily.
- Avoid caffeine and energy drinks, especially in the afternoon and evenings.
- Limit exposure to electronics (computer, cellphone, kindle, etc.) at least an hour before bedtime. Make sure you silence them so you are not tempted to check them during the night.
- Keep your bedroom cool, dark, and quiet.

Talk to a medical professional if sleep deprivation is an ongoing concern impacting your quality of life.

I love falling asleep to the sound of rain.

Afterwards

Congratulations on completing Dr. Gwen's A to Z Self-Care Guide to New Beginnings. You did it! However, this is just the beginning of your self-care journey. Self-care is a life-long commitment. Keep making yourself a priority and doing the things that bring you joy and give you life. I am proud of the work you are doing. You should be too!

I thoroughly enjoyed writing this book. As I started outlining the guide, I thought about how many others were starting over. I hope this book provides motivation and guidance to create your new life. I tried to incorporate something for everyone, no matter what area of self-care you need to improve. We are always learning and growing, and our lives are constantly changing, so adjust your self-care regimen as needed.

Now that you have journeyed from A to Z, I encourage you to add to the list. There is so much more that self-care could cover for each letter. For example, J for *joining a group*; K for *knowledge is power*; S for *saying no*. I am curious to know what you would have chosen for each letter. **Visit Dr. Gwen's Counselor Café website, Facebook, Instagram, or YouTube page and send me a message with feedback.** It would be amazing and greatly appreciated if you would leave a review on Amazon or my website (drgwenscounselorcafe.com) stating what you enjoyed about the book.

You will also find additional helpful resources on the website, such as my blog, where I share even more useful tips, and a shop where self-care items can be purchased.

Peace and Blessings,

Dr. Gwen

   @drgwenscounselorcafe

   @drgwenscounselorcafe

   Dr. Gwen's Counselor Cafe

Reflections

AWARENESS, GROWTH, GOALS

This is an opportunity to write what you learned about yourself, growth opportunities, and future goals.

_____

_____

_____

_____

_____

_____

_____

_____

Keep Going

Keep going and growing. I hope you learned valuable tips, tools, and strategies that will help you as you continue your self-care journey.

Maintain a growth mindset so that you will continue to make improvements personally and professionally. Self-care is an ongoing commitment to being the best, most authentic, happy YOU! Take the information and tips that you learned from this A-to-Z Guide and apply them to every aspect of your life. Then, commit to being just a little bit better each day. Remember, small, consistent changes over time yield BIG results.

> It does not matter how slowly you go as long as you do not stop.
>
> — Confucius

My Commitment

Make a commitment to yourself on how you will continue your self-care journey. Writing your commitment down and sharing it with someone will make it more achievable and you more accountable. Afterward, take the self-care pledge.

_____

_____

_____

_____

_____

_____

_____

_____

_____

Self-Care Pledge

I, _____, promise to RISE, REFLECT and REFORM my life by practicing self-care. I pledge to cultivate habits that uplift ME, reduce stress, and enhance my overall health and well-being. I will take time each day to invest in ME, mind, body, and spirit because I am worth it.

Signed _____

YOU
are worth the
TIME
and
ENERGY!

At the end of every month, take time to complete a self-care wellness check-up to determine if you need to make any adjustments in your daily routines.

	Self-Care Check-Up		
		YES	NO
1.	Are you expressing gratitude daily?		
2.	Are you asking for help and feedback when needed?		
3.	Are you saying YES to new growth opportunities?		
4.	Do you get regular exercise?		
5.	Do you get 7-9 hours of sleep nightly?		
6.	Are you reading for pleasure and information?		
7.	Have you forgiven yourself and others for past mistakes?		
8.	Have you quit bad habits?		
9.	Are you spending quality time with family and friends?		
10.	Are you taking "Me Time"?		
11.	Are you taking deep breaths throughout the day?		
12.	Have you learned a new skill or hobby?		
13.	Are you eating healthy meals?		
14.	Are you using positive self-talk?		
15.	Are you kind and compassionate to yourself and others?		

The greatest
WEALTH
Is
HEALTH!

Acknowledgements

I dedicate this book to my fellow helping professionals. Thank you for using your passion for motivating and inspiring others daily. Your dedication and commitment to servicing communities across the country are appreciated. You are making a difference and changing lives. The world is a better place because of YOU!

Images via Canva & Pixabay.

Book Review

1. What did you like most about the *A-to-Z Self-Care Guide to New Beginnings*?
2. What did you like least about this Guide?
3. What was your favorite affirmation or quote?
4. What feelings did the guide bring to the surface?
5. What did you learn from completing the guide?
6. If you got a chance to ask the author of this guide one question, what would it be?
7. What do you believe was the author's purpose in creating this guide?
8. If you created this guide, what would you add or change?
9. How would you rate the guide on a scale of 1 to 10, with ten being the best?
10. Would you recommend this guide to others? Why or why not?

Meet Dr. Gwen

Gwendolyn A. Martin, who goes by the name Dr. Gwen is a licensed professional counselor, educator, and advocate who is dedicated to spotlighting the importance of self-care in managing and cultivating health and happiness. She is the owner of Dr. Gwen's Counselor Café LLC, a platform that provides effective self-care solutions for educators, including teachers, counselors, licensed clinicians, and other helping professionals. Her professional development trainings, empowerment workshops, speaking engagements, mentoring, consultation, self-care products, and books help people transform their personal and professional lives. When she isn't working, she invests in self-care by spending time with her loved ones, nurturing her garden, cooking healthy vegetarian/pescatarian dishes, and cuddling up with a good romance novel. You can find out more about Dr. Gwen at drgwenscounselorcafe.com.

References

Quotations in this book were obtained from compilation websites. Although every precaution has been taken to verify the accuracy of the quotes, some may contain errors or have been misattributed. The author and publisher assume no responsibility or liability for any errors or omissions consequently for the use and application of any of the contents of this book.

www.brainyquote.com
www.goodhousekeeping.com
www.keepinspiring.me
www.oprahdaily.com
www.positivepsychology.com
www.readersdigest.com
www.therapistaid.com
www.wisdomquotes.com
www.sunnybrook.ca/gethelp

American Heart Association. American Heart Association Recommendations for Physical Activity in Adults and Kids. (2018). Retrieved from https://www.heart.org/en/healthy-living/fitness/fitness-basics/aha-recs-for-physical-activity-in-adults

Hirshkowitz, M., Whiton, K., Albert, S. M., Alessi, C., Bruni, O., DonCarlos, L., Hazen, N., Herman, J., Katz, E. S., Kheirandish-Gozal, L., Neubauer, D. N., O'Donnell, A. E., Ohayon, M., Peever, J., Rawding, R., Sachdeva, R. C., Setters, B., Vitiello, M. V., Ware, J. C., & Adams Hillard, P. J. (2015). National Sleep Foundation's sleep time duration recommendations: Methodology and results summary. Sleep health, 1(1), 40–43. https://pubmed.ncbi.nlm.nih.gov/29073412/

Holt-Lunstad, J., Smith, T. B., & Layton, B. (21). Social relationships and mortality risk: A metaanalytic review. PLoS Medicine, 7(7): e1316. doi:1.1371/journal.pmed.1316

MedlinePlus: National Library of Medicine (US). (2014, April 14). Healthy Sleep. https://medlineplus.gov/healthysleep.html

Rizzolo, Denise & Zipp, Genevieve & Simpkins, Susan & Stiskal, Doreen. (2009). Stress management strategies for students: The immediate effects of yoga, humor, and reading on stress. Journal of College Teaching and Learning. 6. 79-88. 10.19030/tlc.v6i8.1117.

Russo. M. A., Santarelli, D.M., O'rourke D. The physiological effects of slow breathing in the healthy human. Breathe (Sheff). 2017;13(4):298-309. doi:10.1183/20734735.009817

Watson LR, Fraser M. & Ballas P. Journaling for mental health. Health Encyclopedia. University of Rochester Medical Center. Retrieved from https://www.urmc.rochester.edu/encyclopedia/content.aspx?ContentID=4552&ContentTypeID=1

~ Notes ~

~ Notes ~

~ Notes ~

~ Notes ~

Dr. Gwen's Counselor Café LLC
(Additional self-care products available on Amazon or @drgwenscounselorcafe.com/shop)

Made in the USA
Monee, IL
21 September 2024